BLUE PETER SPECIAL ASSIGNMENT
Madrid, Dublin and York

Blue Peter Special Assignment

MADRID:	Film Cameraman	Ray Henman
	Sound Recordist	Ron Brown
	Director	Peter Smith

DUBLIN:	Film Cameraman	Hugh Miles
	Sound Recordist	Ron Brown
	Director	Harry Cowdy

YORK:	Film Cameraman	David Jackson
	Sound Recordist	Dennis Cartwright
	Director	David Brown

| | Research by | Dorothy Smith |
| | Producer | Edward Barnes |

BLUE PETER
SPECIAL ASSIGNMENT

Madrid, Dublin and York

EDWARD BARNES AND DOROTHY SMITH

---

*With fourteen full colour photographs
and with line drawings by Sara Silcock*

A Piccolo Original

PAN BOOKS LTD
LONDON

First published 1974 by Pan Books Ltd,
33 Tothill Street, London SW1
by arrangement with the British Broadcasting
Corporation

ISBN 0 330 23907 6

Also available in Piccolo by
Edward Barnes and Dorothy Smith

BLUE PETER SPECIAL ASSIGNMENT:
Rome, Paris and Vienna
BLUE PETER SPECIAL ASSIGNMENT:
London, Amsterdam and Edinburgh
BLUE PETER SPECIAL ASSIGNMENT:
Venice and Brussels

Made and printed in Great Britain by
Cox & Wyman Ltd, London, Reading and Fakenham

HELLO THERE!

It's getting on for two years since I became Blue Peter's Roving Reporter.

I wouldn't like to count the number of times I've packed and unpacked my suitcase since then, or the number of trains, planes, buses, taxis, trams and boats I've travelled in – not to mention the number of airports, stations, harbours and hotel lobbies I've waited in!

The awful thing about airports and the roads to airports and the international hotels is that they all look exactly the same. Some businessmen travelling around the capitals of Europe say they sometimes forget which city they're in!

But I'm luckier than they are, because on Blue Peter Special Assignments I've tried to find out what's *different* about every city, and to investigate the lives of some of the *extraordinary* people who lived there in the past. I've been able to tread the same stones, sit in the same chairs, and touch the same things as some of the greatest figures in the history of Europe. And I've had the chance to meet some of the famous, and some of the ordinary people who live in the cities today. I also found out some of the strange and quirky things that exist in every city, which people who live there often don't know about.

It's all this that makes the Blue Peter Assignments so special. It's the reason I enjoy them – and I hope that you'll enjoy them too.

Valerie Singleton

MADRID

Arriving in Madrid

It's one of the strangest ways I've ever arrived at a Special Assignment, I thought, looking out from the swinging cabin. I was hanging from an aerial rope-way that was taking me right down into the heart of the city of Madrid. It's called a teleferique, and it was actually built to carry people *out* of the city, rather than bring them in. It takes the Madrilenos – the people of Madrid – swinging over the traffic jams for a Saturday outing in the huge park called the Casa di Campo.

Casa di Campo means Country House, and four hundred years ago King Philip II bought the forest of pine and fir trees for hunting. It was Philip II, too, who made Madrid the Capital of Spain in 1561. Before this the country had been divided into separate kingdoms, but at last they were united, and Philip decided that Madrid, right in the middle of the country, should be its capital.

Today Madrid is a modern city of three and a half

million people, and still growing. Right across, from North to South runs the wide tree-lined Avenue de las Castellana. It was built in the last century, but it has been widened to make room for today's traffic, and new hotels and shops and offices have been built. The thirty-four storey Madrid Tower, Madrid's highest building, looks down on the former Royal Palace.

Not much remains of the insignificant medieval town, or the wild hunting forests that once surrounded the city; but the Madrilenos do remember it all, in one place – their coat of arms. The badge of Madrid is a bear, reaching up to take cherries from a tree, for once there were bears, and wild boar, and even wolves, within a few miles of the city. So you can see the bear and the cherry tree everywhere – on lamp-posts and dust-carts, and official notices, and on the sides of all Madrid's buses and taxis.

The Gypsy Dancers of Spain

You don't see the bear and cherry tree on the vehicles that would have actually been in Madrid when the bears were around – the gypsy caravans! For centuries gypsies have roamed across Spain, and their caravans are still a common sight outside the cities. There is even a special lane reserved for them on some of the busy main roads.

Gypsies have always been a part of the Spanish scene, known everywhere for their singing and dancing. They used to form groups of singers, dancers and guitarists, and play at fairs and markets, and wayside inns. The music they played is called Flamenco. The gypsies didn't invent it, but they *were* responsible for taking it all over Spain, and making it very popular.

Flamenco dancers

It is still a firm favourite, with Spaniards and tourists alike, so I was delighted when my Assignment to Madrid included a visit to a place which claims to have the best Flamenco artistes in the whole country. It was called The Café de Chinitas, and I was told that a table would be reserved for the Blue Peter film crew. If we wanted to see the *first* performance we should be there by half-past midnight.

'I hope we all stay awake,' said Ray Henman, our Australian cameraman.

We normally start filming at eight in the morning, and although the Spanish never seem to go to bed, *we* all tended to be a bit yawny by midnight. But before we ever reached our table, all idea of sleep left my mind!

A beautiful black-haired girl, wearing a white flounced dress, was standing in the centre of the stage. She was motionless in a pool of smoke-filled light. Then there was a sound of fierce rasping chords from the guitars in the blackness, and the girl let out a long low wail that sent shudders down my spine. Another cannonade from the guitar was followed by an even more spine-chilling wail.

'Olé,' someone called softly in the darkness.

Slowly the singer bent her knee and brought her heel down on the step with a crack like a pistol shot. The lights went up, the tempo changed to a wild and furious rhythm. My toes couldn't keep pace with it, but the row of clapping performers, that the lights had revealed sitting at the back of the stage, had no such problem. They clapped in time to the ever increasing tempo until their hands were a blur before their faces.

Suddenly two of them, a girl in a vivid orange dress and a man with dark oily hair, leapt to the front of the stage and began to dance. The stage was tiny, but the couple moved at a ferocious pace, twisting their bodies so furiously that I felt if they moved any faster they would turn themselves inside out! The excitement built up to an almost unbearable pitch.

And then it stopped. The dancers were motionless – and for a split second the whole club froze in a suspended animation of deafening silence.

Then a roar of tremendous applause. I felt sad and excited at the same time. It wasn't until later I discovered that the song was about a tempestuous love affair that had ended in death!

For centuries Spain was ruled over by the Arabs, known then as the Moors, and was part of the world of Mohammedan North Africa. Their rule was strongest in the south, particularly in the province of Andalusia, and it is from there that this strange non-European music stems. Originally the music was never written down, but handed on from father to son, from master to pupil. It is traditional music, but it is a living tradition, with new music and dancing being added all the time.

Everything that struck me about the performance in the Café de Chinitas is part of the Flamenco pattern. It is always original and varied, marked by a great sense of style, and elegance. The music is harsh, with strong rhythms, and musicians and dancers must possess a superb sense of timing.

Flamenco sings of joy and love, but just as often the songs are about sorrow and death:

Since I have seen you, my heart weeps blood;
I wish to die, for my pain is too great . . .

was the translation of one song I heard.

The beautiful sinuous hand and finger movements are essential – there are no formal 'steps' as in the dancing we are used to, only foot and heel movements that beat out the rhythm.

Guitarists always accompany the singing and dancing, while the rest of the troupe mark the rhythm by clapping or snapping their fingers. Always at some stage during the show the guitarists stop being accompanists, and give solo performances. I was very struck by our guitarists, for their playing was extremely exciting, but one of them, who was playing marvellously, was a fair-haired young man, who didn't look Spanish at all.

Afterwards, I met the performers – Luei Peal, the dancer in the orange dress, and her partner, El Camborio. Then the fair guitar player gave a very Spanish bow, as he was introduced. 'This is Ian Davies,' I was told.

'You surely can't be Spanish with a name like that.'

He laughed. 'No, I'm quite English!'

We were all amazed at the idea of an Englishman playing the guitar in Spain, so the Blue Peter crew and I arranged to meet Ian the next day. He had another performance that night, and couldn't stop to talk then. He suggested we should meet for a drink before dinner and when we asked what time, he said, 'Oh, about eight o'clock,' and hurried away.

It sounded very late for a drink *before* dinner, but we had already learnt that meals in Spain are eaten very late indeed. Lunch is usually about two-thirty or three, and dinner is often at ten, or even eleven, at

night. It seems rather odd, and it means that everyone goes to bed late, even the children, and the
streets of Madrid are lively and bustling till two and
three in the morning.

But after work, from about eight o'clock in the
evening onwards, men flock into the bars and cafés,
to drink a glass of wine and to have something to eat.
All the bars serve tit-bits – slices of sausage, bits of
cheese, tomatoes, and pieces of fish, and prawns,
which are the top favourites. They are delicious, but
I can't understand why Madrid, so far from the sea,
is so fond of prawns. Apparently there is a fleet of
refrigerated lorries that brings in fresh fish, nowadays
– but how did it get to be so popular in the first place?
I couldn't work it out at all.

Anyway, it was at a bar serving tapas, which is
what the savoury nibbles are called, that we met Ian
Davies next evening. Ian ordered the drinks and
tapas from the barman, and we walked over to a
quiet table in the window. He spoke Spanish fluently,
and as he spoke his hands made very Spanish
gestures which disappeared as soon as he started to
talk English again.

The first thing I wanted to know was how a tall,
blond, Englishman ended up playing a guitar in a
Spanish night club.

'Well, when I was at Primary School in North
London, it wasn't the Osmonds that all the kids
were screaming for – it was the Beatles! Beatlemania
was at its height; everybody in my school was mad
about the Beatles, and I was no exception. In fact, I
wasn't just mad about them – I wanted to *be* one. So I

decided that the best way to become a Beatle was to learn how to play the guitar.

'I was lucky because one of my friends had a mother who played, so I arranged to have some lessons with her. She turned out to be Spanish, and played *Flamenco* guitar. I wasn't much interested in Flamenco at the time, but I thought at least I'd learn how to hold the thing – and being ten years old at the time, it was nicer than going to a complete stranger.'

'And so you gradually became interested in Flamenco?' I asked.

'Very gradually, and very slowly – but in the end Flamenco kind of took me over – and after a while the Beatles faded into the background.'

'Then what happened?' I asked him.

'I started coming to Spain for holidays with my parents, and whilst I was here I had some lessons from a great Spanish Flamenco player called Serranito.'

'You were still at school then?'

'I was just on the verge of leaving when Serranito cabled me saying if I came over right away there was this job waiting for me.'

'And that was . . .?'

'Three years ago – when I was seventeen.'

'Gosh – so you came straight from school into the night-club?'

'That's right,' he smiled.

'And how long is it since you first started playing the guitar?'

'Just ten years ago'.

I looked down at his right hand, and saw that he had three enormously long finger-nails.

'They're a very important part of my equipment,' he said. 'I'll show you.'

He picked up his guitar and crouched over it. The long talons of his right hand rolled over the strings, as his left hand flashed up and down on the fret. He really did play quite magnificently. In that atmosphere of sherry and tapas in the twilight of a Madrid evening Ian seemed to conjure up all the romance of Spain, which had begun in a primary school in North London, and a yearning to play the guitar like the Beatles!

Philip II and the Enterprise against England

The Spaniards are very aware of their history, and in the Retiro Park, which lies in the centre of Madrid, and was once a royal pleasure garden, I walked along a wide avenue, lined with statues of all the kings and queens of Spain.

Spain was once divided into a dozen kingdoms, but at last, five hundred years ago, the country was united under one ruler. This was the beginning of the Golden Age of Spain, when it was the richest and most powerful country in the world, with a great empire, not only in the Old World of Europe, but in the New World of America as well.

In 1561, King Philip II made Madrid his capital city, but he made no attempt to turn it into a grand and magnificent city; instead, his greatest building achievement was thirty miles away, in the grey rugged Guadarrama mountains.

Here he built the Escorial, a huge, grey monastery as a fitting tomb for his father, the great Emperor Charles V. This majestic gloomy building, half palace and half monastery, was his favourite home. Afterwards it became the tomb for all the kings of Spain.

Philip II

Philip was fascinated by the building, and while it was in progress he would go to a granite nook in the mountains above the Escorial and sit for hours watching the walls rise. The niche is called King Philip's chair to this day.

The monastery itself was dedicated to St Laurence, who was martyred by being burnt on a grid-iron placed over a fire. From the high vantage point, you can see that the building itself is shaped like a grid-iron, standing upside down, with the turrets as its legs and the wings of the building as the cross-bars.

The Escorial is a huge building. It is 676 feet long and 526 feet wide. There are sixteen courtyards, eighty-eight fountains, three chapels, fifteen cloisters,

The Escorial

eighty-six staircases, three hundred rooms, twelve hundred doors and two thousand six hundred and seventy-three windows. It was called the eighth wonder of the world!

But it was not built as a palace but as a monastery, and today there are still monks living in the building.

Philip declared the building was 'to offer respect and honour for death', for, like all Spaniards, he believed that in the midst of life we are in death.

Philip himself was absorbed in religion, and all his actions were sparked off by his religious belief. The Escorial was his power-house, where he came to gather fresh energy, by prayer and by withdrawal from the world. Then he would bring his work here, so that Ministers and foreign ambassadors were obliged to follow him the thirty difficult miles into the mountains. He spent more and more time here, so that the Escorial became his particular creation, marked by his personality.

Philip, as King of Spain, was thought of not as a mere human being, but as the representative of God on earth. When he signed documents he did not write his own name, but 'Yo, el Rey – I, The King.' He had two little daughters, called Catherine and Clara, and it is said that they both stood beside his chair as he wrote, and took it in turns to carry his letters across to his secretary to be sent away.

The library of the Escorial was one of the finest in Europe, but when I walked through it I was amazed to see that all the books were put on the shelves backwards – that is, with the leather bindings inside, and all the pages, with gold-leaf edges, facing outwards. It looked very rich and gleaming, but I felt it would be difficult to find a book in a hurry! In this library, too, there are some magnificent globes of the world, showing the extent of Philip's vast possessions, for he was ruler of Spain, Portugal and the Netherlands, parts of Italy, and the huge empire of Spanish America.

Once he had been King of England too.

When he was twenty-seven years old his father,

Charles V, sent him to England to marry his cousin, thirty-eight year old Mary Tudor, unhappy daughter of Henry VIII and his Spanish Queen Catherine of Aragon. Philip and Mary hoped to make England a Catholic country once more. Mary longed to have a son who would rule after her, but it was not to be.

Mary died, and Philip went back to Spain. Mary's half-sister Elizabeth, Protestant daughter of Anne Boleyn, was crowned Queen of England. She became the implacable enemy of Philip and of Spain. English ships attacked Spanish galleons loaded with treasure from the New World. The formidable Sir Francis Drake assaulted Spanish cities in the West Indies, and held them to ransom.

In the Escorial, in a room called the Hall of the Ambassadors, Philip received the Ministers and high officials who had made the laborious journey from Madrid. When he talked to them, he looked straight into their eyes, which they found very disconcerting.

'Calm yourself,' he would say to his agitated visitors.

He himself was always unemotional. Once a courtier said, 'The King is so calm that he would not move or show the slightest change of expression if he had a cat in his breeches!'

To this room, too, came ambassadors from all the courts of Europe, but probably Philip knew as much about their countries as they did, for his secret service was incredible, with agents everywhere. The reports from his secret agents with information about all the most important people in his vast realms were taken straight through to Philip's private study.

'Here in this room,' people said, 'the King rules the world from two inches of paper.'

The study, left just as it was in Philip's day, is furnished very simply, with only a writing desk and chairs, but as he suffered from gout he had a small stool to rest his leg and ease the agonizing pain.

He dressed plainly, in black doublet and hose, with the Order of the Golden Fleece round his neck.

He worked very hard, and never seemed to get tired.

'No secretary in the world uses more paper than His Majesty', the Court Officials complained.

Even in the austere Escorial, Philip could not escape his court officials, so he used to go back to King Philip's Chair, his own special place on the granite hillside, and from there, solitary and undisturbed, he surveyed his headquarters. It was from this place that Philip planned his greatest scheme – the Enterprise against England.

It was to be a crusade – a Holy War. England was to be invaded by Spanish troops who would occupy the country and force Elizabeth to give up her throne. Then Philip would be proclaimed as King of England and the country would once more be enclosed in the Catholic Church.

The scheme was for a mighty fleet of Spanish ships to leave Spain, and sail along the English Channel, sweeping aside any English ship that tried to halt them. In the Low Countries the fleet would pick up an army of seasoned troops, then turn to attack the South Coast and the Thames Estuary.

It would be a hazardous business, needing very careful preparation, but Philip was a skilful planner, and he was certain this was God's work.

At last, in July 1588, the great Spanish Armada sailed, a hundred and twenty ships with ten thousand sailors. Now they were committed to the Enterprise – they were out of Philip's hands. He could only wait for news, and pray.

He must have watched and waited for many long hours. It was months before he had any news at all. But whilst Philip waited, nearly a thousand miles away the English were preparing for the great Armada.

Francis Drake, the story says, was playing bowls on Plymouth Hoe when he got the news that the ships of Spain were only fifty miles off.

'We have time enough to finish the game, and beat the Spaniards too,' he declared. But when they took to their ships, and sailed out, they found the Spanish ships already in battle formation.

The English ships were light and manoeuvrable, and they sailed between the great galleons. The English gunners were experienced men, and they poured cannonades into the tall ships looming over them.

The Spanish line broke, and the Armada sailed eastward along the Channel, with the English ships continually harrying them. A week later they had reached harbour at Calais.

Then, at midnight, a deadly peril struck them – fire-ships!

Small ships without crews were packed with kindling and pitch, and then, alight and blazing, were set to drift among the Spanish ships, scattering sparks

and firebrands. Discipline was shattered – the proud ships stampeded in a panic to reach the open sea.

There, the English fleet was waiting for them, and they were engaged in a disastrous battle.

And then a violent south-westerly gale sprang up. All that was left of the Invincible Armada was driven into the North Sea, to struggle homeward to Spain, round the North of Scotland and past the West Coast of Ireland.

'God blew with his winds, and they were scattered,' declared the exultant English.

Across England the bells rang out joyfully. The Queen attended a Thanksgiving Service in St Paul's Cathedral. Now Elizabeth had the world in her grasp. She was Gloriana, the triumphant Protestant heroine. Yet she was grudging and avaricious in victory; the English fleet had conquered, but it lay in harbour, the seamen sick and despairing in their ships, for the Queen refused to pay them.

Meanwhile, the defeated Armada struggled through stormy seas, tossed by the waves or wrecked on unfriendly coasts. Philip waited for two months without certain news. It was not until early September, when the arid Spanish countryside lay under the early autumn sunshine, that the messengers arrived. They toiled up the hillside, bringing their master the worst news he was ever to hear.

He blamed no one.

'I sent you to fight against men, not against the wind and waves,' he said.

He pitied those seamen and soldiers who managed to get back, and he treated them generously. Patiently he set to work again, still hoping to destroy Protestant England but it was impossible. More than a hundred years of savage religious wars lay ahead for Europe.

Philip was an old man now, aged by cares and disappointments. He never knew that Spain would soon dwindle from the mighty empire he had ruled, for only a few years were left to him.

Much of his time he spent in bed, in the simple room next to his study, where there was a window looking down over the great church in the Escorial. He thought a great deal about death, and beside his bed he had placed a skull wearing a golden crown, to remind him constantly that even kings must die.

And at last he died, in his plain bedroom in the

23

Escorial, listening to the monks singing Mass in the church below.

The Spanish Bullfight

The biggest open square in Madrid is called the Plaza Mayor, the Great Square – and it is still surrounded by seventeenth century buildings. There are taverns and restaurants close by, and on Sunday morning there is a Stamp Market, for eager philatelists of every age, hoping for a bargain that the sharp-eyed dealers have missed.

The Plaza Mayor was the great place for spectacle. The Royal family, with the Court, and the nobility would take their places at the windows and the balconies and the ordinary people would crowd in close to the buildings all around. And then under the Spanish sun they would all watch whatever was happening – religious ceremonies, and fiestas, pageants, executions, tournaments and bullfights.

Originally there were no specially built bullrings, the Spanish used whatever space came to hand, usually the biggest public square in the town – that is why the Plaza Mayor was Madrid's first bullring.

In those days bullfights were not professional entertainments; they were very aristocratic affairs, with members of the nobility, and sometimes royalty, too, showing off their skill and daring in the beautiful style of riding called Spanish High School. The mounted aristocrats pitted their skill and horsemanship against the bulls, and their servants on foot stood by to give assistance, and to hand them fresh spears.

Sometimes a mounted spearsmen, called a rajonidor, appears in Spanish bullrings today, but it is not
common. In the eighteenth century there was a new
royal family in Spain, who came from France; they
disliked bullfighting, so the nobility gradually stopped
taking part. The bullfight was taken over by the foot
servants, the grooms and the cowboys. The old
aristocratic bullfight came to an end, and for a while
it became a terrible bloodthirsty business, with the
fighters showing off for money, and the whole crowd
taking part in killing the bull. Frequently the whole
crowd would get out of hand.

So the authorities stepped in – a new kind of bullfight developed, with its own rules. It is probably
debased and commercialized from the original, but it
is tremendously popular with many of the Spanish,
and with many of their foreign visitors.

English people have often been rather disturbed at
the idea of a bullfight. In 1793, when Admiral Nelson
was in Spain, he was taken to a great ceremonial bullfight. He wrote home saying he did not greatly enjoy
it, because, 'I felt for the bulls and the horses.'

The great thing to remember, say the enthusiasts,
is that it is not a sport, but a spectacle, or even a play,
with a plot, the actors having set roles. It is an ordeal
by courage – the matador, the bullfighter, has to
master his own fear before he can master the bull. It
all ends in death, and to the Spaniard, traditionally,
this is right and proper, for life ends in death, and
death is important, not just a regrettable accident.

It seems very strange to us, but it is certainly part
of the way of life in Spain, where there are four

hundred and ten bullrings. It is big business, too, with a great deal of money involved. So many bulls are needed, that ranches have been set up all over the country.

I went to one ranch, kept by a former very famous rajonidor, retired from the ring, and now breeding bulls.

The Spanish have a world-wide reputation as horsemen. There were cowboys in Spain long before Columbus discovered America. The greatest High School team in the world may come from Vienna, but it is still called the 'Spanish' Riding School, because their horses originally came from Spain.

When I visited the Spanish Riding School, on my Assignment to Vienna, I was not allowed to mount one of their horses, but at the Cortijo Wellington Ranch, just outside Madrid, I rode with the owner, Don Balthazar Iban, across the rolling plains on a pure bred Palomino stallion.

There are still cowboys in Spain; they are called vaqueros, and, with Don Balthazar, I watched them rounding up a herd of bulls. These were no steers, but prize fighting bulls in the pink of condition. The vaqueros deal with death behind the scenes of the bullfight. For them there are no cheers, no fanfares, no cries of 'Olé' – nothing but dust and a thousand thundering hooves, as they drive the bulls into the corral – and that, too, is a Spanish word!

Don Balthazar explained to me that his bulls are all bred for the 'Corrida' – the bullring.

'So they are all going to be killed eventually,' I asked through the blinding cloud of dust.

'Yes – but of course you could say the same about a

herd of bulls in England – or anywhere in the world, for that matter.'

Don Balthazar explained that according to the law, the bulls must be four years old before they are sent to the bullfight. I asked him if the bulls were trained for the bullring.

He laughed, and said, 'No, you cannot train a bull – they behave quite naturally!'

Vaqueros

'So you don't know until the bull goes into the ring whether he will be any good or not?'

He smiled and looked at the Blue Peter camera that was filming us.

'It's just like your films,' he said. 'Some turn out very good – others, maybe, not so good!'

The corral is a series of pens connected by corridors, and sealed off from each other by portcullis-like doors. Once the bulls are driven into the first pen, and the door dropped behind them, Don Balthazar and his men watch the way they behave, from high narrow walkways surrounding the pen, and then select the bull to be sent away for a particular fight.

I had thought it was dusty out on the plain, but the dense acrid cloud kicked up by fifty snorting bulls in a confined space is beyond description. The cowboys on the galleries have long poles that reach down into the pens, and single out the bull that Don Balthazar selects. When they get him close to the door, there is a great shout, the door is hauled up and the cowboy gives the bull a quick jab that sends him stamping into the next pen. The door falls with a crash behind the bull, isolating him from the rest of the herd.

Up till this moment, I'd enjoyed myself; the ride over the plain and the sight of the splendid bulls – but seeing that confused animal alone in the pen, about to make his last journey to the bullring, suddenly upset me.

As well as feeling sorry for the bull, I thought about the man who would face him alone in the arena in just a few hours time. What makes people want to watch a man risk death in order to kill a bull with a sword?

Later on that day, I drove through the Casa di Campo and there I came upon a group of boys who would have thought that was a stupid question. They were playing bullfights. One of them was the matador, who stood implacably holding out his cape, while his friend, holding a wicker bull's head, charged towards him. The rest stood by, cheering and criticizing with great expertise.

Yet this was not just playing, but a concentrated serious game, with the 'matador' working out all the moves and passes of a star performer. If one of those boys really does become a professional, and makes the grade, he will be feted and adored like a pop-idol – and nearly as rich. A top class matador gets nearly £2,000 for an afternoon's work – which means fighting two bulls.

One matador once was asked if he was afraid of being hurt by the bulls. 'Not so much as I am of being hungry!' he said.

The bullring in Madrid holds over twenty thousand excited spectators or 'aficionados' (enthusiasts), and curious foreign tourists. Outside the ring, in the corridors, there is eager expectancy, and a tremendous sense of atmosphere building up. People sell drinks, and flowers, and programmes, and hire out cushions. Inside, everything is strictly controlled, under the powerful eye of the President of the Day, who is often the Chief of Police. Bullfights always start on time, so that the bullfighters won't have to wait, tense and keyed up, beyond the proper time. Unkind people say that bullfights are the only events that start on time in all Spain!

When the President gives the signal, by waving a white handkerchief, two horsemen in seventeenth century costume ride in, like heralds. They are the President's representatives in the ring – the President indicates when each new stage is to begin, by signals. The heralds are given the key of the gate of the ring;

they unlock the gates, then lead in a parade of all the men who will take part.

First come the matadors, colourful and gleaming in the special costume known as a Suit of Lights. There are three matadors, and they are followed by the members of their own squad, or cuadrilla – the banderilleros, on foot, and the picadors, on horseback, all gaily dressed in silk and velvet. They are followed by the ring attendants, then last of all come men leading a mule that will at the end pull the dead bull away – a rather grim contrast with the colourful procession that goes before it.

Matador in his Suit of Lights

The line files away – the first cuadrilla remains in the ring.

The gates of the pen are opened – and a great bull comes thundering out. Sometimes he is aggressively angry, sometimes bemused and dazed by his strange surroundings. The banderilleros wave capes at him, to interest and excite him, and make him run across the ring towards them. Then they hastily take refuge behind the barrier – this is all to let the matador watch the bull, and study his style and temperament.

Then the matador takes the ring, holding an enormous cape of heavy pink silk, lined with bright yellow. He moves his cape, and directs the bull towards it. He doesn't move his feet but keeps to one place in the ring, using only the upper half of his body. It is rather like the flamenco dancing, and there is something exciting about all this, when the matador shows skill and grace and bravery, and the bull is strong and fresh and full of fight.

The crowd love it; they admire the man and the bull, and they shout, 'Olé, olé' with enormous fervour. But the fight goes on. At the beginning it is strange and beautiful and exciting, but ten minutes later the bull is killed, and the men and the horses may be hurt, or even killed, as well.

I had heard that many Spaniards were against bull-fighting, and I was interested to hear what they had to say. However, it was difficult to find anyone who was prepared to say anything at all. The Government in Spain likes bullfighting, and most Spaniards believe that whilst it may not be necessary to like it as well, it's certainly wiser not to dislike it openly!

Eventually I heard, through a friend of a friend, that one girl *was* prepared to come and put the bull's point of view, in front of the Blue Peter cameras. Even then, she proved to be very elusive, and after several cancelled appointments we had almost given up hope. Then, one afternoon she suddenly appeared on the steps of the Royal Palace, after we thought we had finished filming for the day.

I don't know why, but we had all expected a rather severe elderly lady, so imagine our surprise when a very pretty young girl came up to me, and said, 'Are you the English lady who wanted to talk about bullfights?'

I asked her how strong the anti-bullfight feeling was in Spain. 'I wouldn't call it an anti-feeling; more a lack of interest, especially in the big cities.'

'But they are still enthusiastic in the villages?'

'Yes. You see, it's almost the only entertainment they have. And – I don't know how you say it – they think it's brave, and they don't consider the animals at all – only how brave the fellow is who fights them. It's the glory that interests them.'

I asked her why she thought bullfighting survived in the big cities.

'Well, you know, everybody who comes to Spain wants to see a bullfight. It's the tourists who really keep the corrida alive. They may go back to their own country and say how horrible it was, but without their money it would be difficult to keep the bullfights going. And I must admit there are many people here, both big people and little people, who are living on this thing.

'When you go to the bullfight, you don't see many young Spanish people there.'

'What are they interested in, then?' I asked.

'All kinds of things – music and dancing, and sport. Bullfighting is not a sport. Some people call it an art, but I don't think it's an art either. Young people are interested in real sport, like football, for instance. Have you ever seen Real Madrid playing?'

I told her I hadn't, and then I asked her if *she* had ever been to a bullfight.

'Once, many years ago, before I realized it was such a terrible thing – such a cruel thing. Then I made it a point not even to appear at the fiesta. Not even one of my pesetas is going to that!'

The Princes and Princesses of Spain

In Madrid's Royal Armoury I looked at some tiny suits of armour that had been made for little boys, particularly for the royal princes of Spain. It was difficult to imagine an active small boy in armour, for however well the armourer had made it, it must have been rigid and constricting.

But the Spanish princes hardly led a normal life, for their daily lives were so hedged around with all the limitations of the strict and formal etiquette of the Court of Spain.

Even when they were not put into armour, the royal children were dressed in stiff brocades and silks, so that they could never play or run about. They always had to look like grownups, and behave like grownups, too.

I saw a picture of Prince Balthazar Carlos, who lived three hundred and fifty years ago, painted when he was about four years old. He wears heavy stiff petticoats down to his ankles, but he has a sword, and a staff and a sash of office, just like a general.

His sister looks like a little doll, in her portrait, with a fan, and ribbons and long full skirts. You can't imagine her running or laughing, but Spanish princesses were not supposed to run or laugh!

Their father, King Philip IV – a grandson of Philip II – was kind, but remote, feeling that he was powerless to alter the stiff formal etiquette of his court. He became king when he was sixteen. He could hardly ever take decisions on his own – but once he did make up his own mind, and appointed a Court Painter!

The painter was called Diego Velasquez. He was an artist of twenty-three when he first met King Philip of Spain. The two men became friends, and over the years Velasquez painted revealing portraits of the king and his family. Many of these marvellous pictures are now in the Prado, the magnificent art gallery of Madrid.

Velasquez left us not only some of the greatest pictures in the world, but he recorded forever a glimpse into the lives of the royal family of Spain. He showed Philip as a hunter, out in the countryside with his gun and his dog – and Prince Balthazar Carlos, his son, had to be shown in the same way, a grownup like his father, though the little prince never got out of the palace into the open air!

Philip was portrayed on a great rearing horse (he was a splendid horseman) dressed like a general, and looking every inch a king. Little Balthazar must be a mounted general, too, riding a favourite pony his uncle had given him, though that picture is an illusion as well, for the pony had died, and Philip had ordered it to be stuffed for the portrait.

But Velasquez was a painter; he was not born a courtier, and he was able to see his sitters as real people under their formal robes, whether he was painting Spanish royalty, or their attendants.

The royal family, strange though it sounds, liked to surround themselves with dwarfs, and unfortunate mis-shapen people, and these were chosen to be companions for the royal children. 'Men of pleasure' they were called – and Velasquez painted the men and women inside the twisted bodies with kindness and truth, just as he painted the dressed up princes and princesses of Spain, those pale, frail little creatures who seemed haunted by the ghosts of their own ancestors who lay in the crypt of the Escorial.

As Velasquez painted him over the years Philip grew old. He was burdened with the cares of his country, and sunk in gloom. His son Prince Balthazar Carlos died, and for many years there was no heir to the throne. His wife was hard and selfish, trapped in the rigorous court etiquette she no longer wished to escape.

In the end their only happiness came from their little daughter. Margarita, she was called, a pretty fair-haired little girl. For a moment she warmed the frozen court, and inspired Velasquez to paint his greatest picture. It shows a scene in Velasquez's palace studio, the walls lined with pictures. The artist stands at his easel, holding his palette exactly as he always did. He is painting the king and queen. They are outside the picture, but they can be seen in the mirror that hangs at the far end of the studio. To amuse them while they stand, the little Princess Margarita has come to the studio with her own attendants. One of her maids of honour is kneeling to offer her a drink of water – her attendants always had

to kneel down when they gave her anything. Another is curtseying to her. Clustered round her are her dog, her dwarfs, her governess, her escort.

It is a painting about a painting, which gives you as you look at it the feeling of eavesdropping on a moment of life in that strange court, saved for us out of time.

The Family was the name the Spanish royal family themselves used to call it, but now it is always known as *Las Meninas – the Maids of Honour*.

Perhaps that painting is the greatest achievement of Philip IV's long reign. As a ruler he was a failure, but by appointing Velasquez as his Court Painter he left more to the world than many greater kings of Spain.

When he died, Philip IV, like all the kings and queens of Spain, was taken to the Royal Crypt at the Escorial. It lies beneath the church, directly under the High Altar that Philip II was able to watch from his bed. It is a gloomy, splendidly decorated room, rich with gold and dark marble.

In coffins round the room, neatly arranged in date order, lie all the kings and queens of Spain. Kings are on one side – I read the name of Philip II, and his father Charles V, and Philip IV. On the other side are the queens whose sons became kings. Other royal ladies, and mere princes and princesses, have a less splendid resting place in a room beyond.

Today it is a tourist attraction, and people from all over the world queue up to see the coffins that house the earthly remains of the men who once controlled the mighty Spanish Empire.

It seemed a bit spooky to think of the Spanish royal family in the Escorial living on top of their own graveyard, but in a way it's appropriate, because the Spanish have always accepted death as a part of life, as well as its end.

It shows in their music, their history, their bullfights, and even in their exciting dance of flamenco, there's more than a hint of death!

DUBLIN

The Waters of the Liffey

Dublin is famous for stout – famous for making it and famous for drinking it!

The pint is the staple diet of most male Dubliners, and the pub where they drink it used to be a jealously guarded male preserve. Today the pub is the centre of social life for men and women, and coffee and all sorts of other drinks are served besides stout.

The Irishman, and the Dubliner in particular, has always been a great storyteller, a great singer, and a great downer of pints, so the first night I was in Dublin I went to Mulligan's in Poolbeg Street, near the quayside, to listen to some of the stories, and to hear Bob Lynch sing some of his songs. And to try my first pint of fiery black beer . . .

'You've never drunk stout until you've tried it in Dublin,' is what the stout connoisseurs say. Well, I didn't mind the thick layer of froth on top, but you can keep the black stuff that goes underneath it!

The pub, though, was a great place. Bob sang all

kinds of Irish songs – funny songs, sad songs, songs of passion, songs of love and songs of hate. All of them told a story, and many of them were set in Dublin.

> *At the age of seventeen*
> *I was 'prenticed to a grocer,*
> *Not far from* Stephen Green
> *Where Miss Henny used to go, sir* . . .

and another more sombre one:

> *The Four Courts of Dublin*
> *The British bombarded,*
> *The spirit of freedom*
> *They tried hard to quell.*

And another was about Dublin's river, the Liffey.

> *We wandered by Thomas Street down to the Liffey*
> *The sunshine was gone so the evening grew dark,*
> *Along by King's Bridge and begod in a jiffey*
> *Me arm was round her beyant in the park.*

The black stout is often called Liffey Water, but I was assured it is really made from a fresh spring just outside Dublin, which is piped into the city especially for the brewery. I was very relieved to hear that, because, lovely as Dublin's river looked, I'm not sure I'd have liked to drink its water.

The River Liffey flows through the heart of Dublin – it reminded me of my visit to Paris, and the Seine. It's broad and majestic with great trees along its banks, and wide bridges, twelve of them in all. The Liffey, more than anything else, has led to Dublin being called the Paris of the North.

But that's not the only thing the two cities have in common. Dublin, like Paris, has many broad, stately, tree-lined streets. The most famous is O'Connell

O'Connell Street

Street, with shops, banks and cinemas and along its centre a row of statues to Irish patriots and statesmen. Half way down is the General Post Office, with its huge classical portico, a building that once played an important part in Ireland's history.

Dublin has many fine shops and restaurants, with all the sophistication of a modern European capital and, like Paris, Dublin has a huge traffic problem. Although it's not so noisy, the traffic seems just as dense as it winds round a maze of one way streets. Many people prefer to find their way round the city on foot, and one of the bridges over the Liffey is a footbridge, reserved for pedestrians. It's called the Halfpenny Bridge, because of a toll levied on it long ago.

Just as in Britain the old halfpenny has disappeared from the coinage, so it has in Ireland, for Irish money was decimalized at the same time as the British. In

Ireland you can use either British or Irish coins – the Irish ones are the same size and shape but otherwise quite different – most of them have animals on one

side and all the animals have some particular significance. The fivepence has a bull because agriculture is so important to Ireland; the tenpence piece has a salmon, the ancient Irish symbol of wisdom; the fifty pence piece has a woodcock, because this wild, shy game bird is the favourite of all Irish sportsmen and the copper coins all have legendary birds copied from old Celtic manuscripts.

And when you turn the coins over, you see that they all carry the picture of a harp. The harp is the national symbol of the country, so it's not surprising that you see it all over the city, on buses and notices and coats-of-arms, as well as on the coins.

In the Irish language, Dublin is called Baile Atha Claithe; the name literally means 'town with a ford of hurdles' and it dates from even before Dublin's first settlers, the Vikings. These invaders from Scandinavia were attacking England, Scotland and Northern France as well as Ireland during the eighth and ninth centuries, and when they decided to settle by the Liffey, during the ninth century, they looked for a river crossing to start their simple community.

Over the centuries the settlement grew to a town, and the town to Dublin City and today you can still find Viking names among the street signs in some parts of the town; Olaf Road and Northman Place, Thor Place and Viking Place.

But all over Ireland, as well as Dublin, signposts and notices on public buildings are in Irish as well as in English. The Irish language is spoken in parts of Ireland, but I didn't hear it much in Dublin where even most of the songs I heard were sung in English.

Molly Malone and Grace O'Malley

In Dublin's Fair City,
Where the girls are so pretty,
There lived an old lady called Molly Malone.
She wheeled her wheelbarrow
Through streets broad and narrow,
Crying, 'Cockles and mussels, alive, alive-o.'

Most people have heard that song, and in Dublin I walked down the street where Molly Malone wheeled her wheelbarrow. It's called Moore Street, and it's one of Dublin's main markets, slap in the middle of the city. It bustles with people and they sell every kind of vegetable, but I'm afraid I didn't see anyone selling cockles and mussels. There were several old ladies with old wooden wheelbarrows, which haven't changed since the days of Molly Malone, but no shellfish.

Molly Malone herself was a very poor old lady who lived a couple of hundred years ago and who has become something of a legendary figure. She sold her cockles and mussels during the day from a stall in Moore Street, and to theatregoers during the evening, and that was how she came to be so well known. Though she was such a familiar figure at the stage doors of Dublin's theatres, Molly Malone remained poor and miserable all her life. Then, one winter morning, she was found dead, her body huddled beside her cockle wheelbarrow.

Now her ghost wheels her wheelbarrow,
Through streets broad and narrow . . .

43

Molly Malone used to go to Howth, the harbour on the edge of Dublin, to stock up her wheelbarrow with cockles and mussels. Today Howth is still a small port, and a very attractive one, busy with boats and fishermen. It's a natural harbour set in the coast of a rocky peninsula just to the north of the city.

The Howth peninsula helps to form the great curve of Dublin Bay, and it's a historic part of Dublin. The descendants of the Norman Lords who invaded long ago still live there at Howth Castle. They conquered the peninsula in 1177, and Sir Almeric Tristam who won the battle changed the family name to St Lawrence because it was fought on St Lawrence's day. For centuries Howth castle has been the home of the St Lawrence family. It's a fine building with many old tales connected with it.

I was invited by the present Mr St Lawrence to call on him and hear one of the strangest stories about the castle. He told me that nearly four hundred years ago, at the time of the Spanish Armada in 1588, a woman called Grace O'Malley lived on the West Coast of Ireland. She was a kind of pirate queen who existed by robbing and plundering ships sailing off the coast.

When the Spanish Armada scattered in complete disorder after being routed by the English some of the ships were wrecked off the Irish coast. Grace O'Malley fell on them, killed the survivors and got away with a great deal of loot. When Elizabeth I in England heard of this she was grateful and invited her to Court in England to be formally thanked. On her way back Grace O'Malley was nearly shipwrecked, so she put into Dublin Bay and demanded refuge at Howth Castle. She was refused. Furiously angry, she seized the heir to the St Lawrence family as a hostage, and once more demanded food and drink. This time, she was not refused.

When she left the castle, Grace O'Malley demanded that an extra place should evermore be laid at the table for her, or for any other unexpected O'Malley guest. She also insisted that the gate of the castle should always be left open.

After he had told me this extraordinary story, Mr St Lawrence led me into the family dining room. The table had been cleared, except for the cruets but there, at the head of the table, just one place was set.

'I'm sorry,' apologized Mr St Lawrence, 'The extra place hasn't been cleared away since lunch.'

'So there's never been a time when you have had breakfast or lunch or dinner here that you haven't laid that extra place?'

'No, never!'

'Do you know if any of your ancestors ever forgot to lay the place?'

'To the best of my knowledge, it's always been laid, and the gates have always been kept open. And it's gone on for generations.'

I asked him why they always did it.

'Grace O'Malley put a curse on the heir of the family, if the place was not laid. I wouldn't be prepared to see an accident happen to my son because we hadn't laid the extra place.'

'So you really take it seriously?' I asked.

'Yes, we do,' said Mr St Lawrence firmly, 'And I

45

think you would, if you were in the same position.'

Hurling

'It's Mick Crotty from Mossie Murphy – housted by Pa Dillon, but Kilkenny must score!'

The roar from the packed stadium was as deafening as anything heard at Wembley. This was an All Ireland Cup Final, but it wasn't football, and it wasn't rugby; it wasn't even Irish football. It was hurling – Ireland's great national sport.

It looks like hockey at first, but when you see the players race down the pitch hitting the ball up and down their sticks all the way to the goal mouth, you realize that there's quite a difference.

Hurling is played by everyone in Ireland, in great stadiums, school sports grounds, and the back streets of Dublin, by men, women, and children. The only difference is the girls' game has got a different name – it's called camogie, though no one could tell me why!

I had a go at camogie with the girls of The Presentation School and the Mount Carmel School one Saturday afternoon in Phoenix Park in Dublin. It was fairly disastrous, which won't be surprising to anyone who knows about me and ball games! However, I did learn that you can hit the ball *through* the goal, or *over* the post; that you can pick the ball up and run with it for three paces; and that there is no off-side rule.

Oh – and guess what the ball's called. It's called a schlitter.

Parts of Dublin, like so many other cities, are being re-developed, and old buildings are being pulled down to make way for new ones.

Ten years ago the Dublin authorities planned a new Civic Centre, right in the middle of the city, at the corner of High Street and Wine Tavern Street. When the work of digging the foundations was well under way, some interesting discoveries were made. Soon it was realized that by accident they had stumbled on the remains of Dublin's first Viking settlement.

Building was suspended, and the new work, of digging up the past was given to archaeologist Brendan O'Riordan. To help him he was allowed to use some of the council's workmen – men who usually worked on the roads or as builders' labourers. Some of these men have worked on the site for ten summers, going back to their ordinary work in the winter. Though untrained, they soon became very expert and very excited by all their discoveries, and their continuous work on the site has really been more valuable than students or part-time helpers who can only give two or three weeks at a time.

I was taken round the site by Brendan O'Riordan, who explained everything to me. It was very strange to go inside a wooden fence, and look over a patch of earth, carefully smoothed and measured, and partly covered by plastic sheets, knowing that a thousand years ago this was a Viking village.

Twelve hundred years ago, barbarian tribes swept

over Europe, burning houses and churches, destroying everything. These years were called the Dark Ages, but in those terrible days Ireland stood for culture and civilization. St Patrick went to Ireland and converted the Irish to the Christian faith – books were written, and wonderful works of art were created.

One of the loveliest is a beautiful silver cup. It is known as the Ardagh Chalice, and was used to hold wine for the most sacred services of the church. It is decorated with bands of gold in a lace pattern called filigree. Set in the bands are studs of blue and red

The Ardagh Chalice

glass, and round the stem are traced the names of the twelve apostles. Right underneath, where no one could see it, there is set a beautiful sparkling rock crystal.

In the Court of the Kings at the Escorial

The Escorial – Philip II's granite headquarters

The statue of Velasquez outside the **Prado Art Gallery**

Filming in Dublin

Molly Malone's Street

Mount Carmel School gives me a hurling lesson

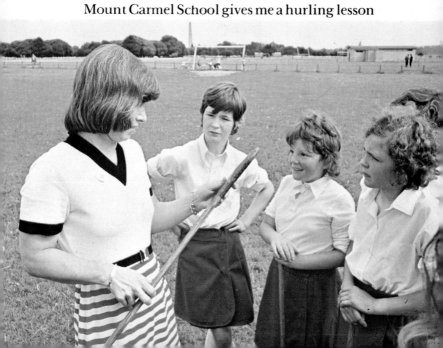

A Viking Wine Jar found on a building site

The Ardagh Chalice

The GPO where the Republic was first proclaimed

James Brennan showing me his cell in Kilmainham Jail

JAMES J. BRENNAN 1916

Outside York Minster

In Castle Museum

Filming in the Museum

Walking down the Shambles – one of the oldest streets in York

The Ardagh Chalice is certainly a wonderful example of the metalworker's art, but the greatest of all Irish treasures is not an object in silver or gold, but a book. It is the Book of Kells, and it is kept in Dublin's Trinity College. It has been called the most beautiful book in the world. It is a manuscript of the four Gospels, worked in decorated writing by Celtic monks twelve hundred years ago. It is written in Latin, and many of the pages are covered in the most delicately coloured and incredibly detailed Celtic designs. The first few words of each chapter are on a page to themselves, and the very first letter is made the basis of the swirling intricate pattern. My favourite page showed the symbols of the four writers of the

From the Book of Kells

Gospels – a Man for Matthew, a Winged Lion for Mark, a Bull for Luke, and an Eagle for John.

The book was started by Irish monks working in a monastery on the Island of Iona off Scotland, probably around the year AD 706. In the middle of the work the Island was invaded by Vikings and the monks were driven away. They fled to Ireland, taking the half-finished book with them, and they established a new monastery at a place called Kells.

Eventually the monks finished their masterpiece. The new monastery was also attacked, but the precious manuscript survived and remained there until 1653, when it was sent to Dublin and given to Trinity College.

Today the Book of Kells is regarded as a symbol of Ireland's civilization, glowing in the midst of the Dark Ages. It is one of Europe's finest treasures.

The Library itself is a very fine and stately place, and I thought it was splendid that Dubliners could just walk in to see their most cherished possession.

A Weird Dublin Story

Of course there is a constant flow of visitors to see the Book of Kells in Trinity College Library. Another spot in Dublin that draws crowds of people, for very different reasons, is a little church called St Michan's.

In the churchyard, I met curator Harold Wilmot. He took me to the side of the church, unlocked an iron door with a huge key, and showed me a steep flight of steps. I felt as if I was really going down into the depths of the earth. When we reached the crypt that lies beneath the church, Harold Wilmot told me the strange story, just as he tells it to all the hundreds of visitors who come to St Michan's every year.

In the vaults numerous coffins are lodged – and he shone a torch, showing dull brass, heavy dark wood, and solid metal. All the coffins were covered with dust, and festooned with cobwebs. I could well understand that when Irish writer Bram Stoker saw the place, he was inspired to go away and write his creepy thriller *Dracula*!

It is a scientific fact that the limestone rock strata in which the crypt is built has a peculiar drying effect, so that the bodies inside those coffins are in a perfect state of preservation. But there are two famous exceptions, and this was the point of Harold Wilmot's story.

'In 1798,' he said, 'there was a rebellion in Ireland. Two patriots were executed, and their coffins were lodged in the tombs under St Michan's. There they stayed for a hundred years, and their bodies were preserved like all the other bodies lying under St Michan's Church. Then, one day, to commemorate the hundredth anniversary of the patriots' deaths, someone brought in a bunch of flowers, and laid it on their coffins.' Mr Wilmot pointed to the flowers as he spoke – a black, shrivelled crumbling bunch of dry twigs. 'But there was something strange about those flowers, because immediately the two bodies began to decompose, and to crumble into dust! They took out the remains and put them in fresh coffins, and there they remain to this day.'

'How fantastic!' I exclaimed. 'What was the reason?'

'Well,' Mr Wilmot began to explain, 'it must have been some bacteria on the flowers. It can act very quickly. It must have spread right through the vault, and then the bodies decayed.'

'Were the bodies in the other vaults affected?' I asked.

'Oh, no, they stayed just as they had always been.'

'What did people say at the time? Did they realize it was bacteria?'

'They certainly did not. They thought the flowers were bewitched, and that they cast a spell on the bodies. And there's many folk who think so still!'

The Protestant Ascendancy

I was very glad to get out of the gloomy, creepy vaults under the church and into the sunshine, but before I went away altogether, I went to have a look in the church itself. Not many visitors do that, and I think this is a pity, because it's very interesting.

St Michan prides itself on having a very fine organ, where a celebrated musician played. His name was George Frederick Handel, and Dublin has a famous connection with him, for it was in the Musick Hall, in Dublin (since pulled down), that his great work the *Messiah* was first performed in 1742. Today the *Messiah* is often performed with enormous choirs of hundreds of men and women, but in Handel's day large bodies of singers were rare, so he scored the *Messiah* for the combined choirs of two cathedrals –

they numbered in all fourteen men and six boys. Even so, the first performance of the choir delighted the audience, and moved the critics to raptures.

I looked at the carved wooden organ, with its elegant gilded decorations, and the ranks of pipes in every size, and I could imagine Handel playing there, crashing out the mighty chords of the Hallelujah Chorus.

At the time that he was playing, much of the finest building in Dublin was being planned. In the eigh-

Handel

teenth century Dublin and Ireland were ruled by Anglo-Irish Protestants and the Irish Catholics were oppressed.

The Protestants built themselves fine houses and set up a commission to build wide, stately streets. In dignified Georgian mansions on Merrion Square lived eminent physicians, barristers and writers. Dublin presented an appearance of peace and prosperity for two centuries, and seemed to be as fine a capital as any in Europe.

But while handsome Protestant churches were built, severe restrictions were imposed on building churches for Roman Catholics – and most of the Irish people were Roman Catholics. In the countryside poor Catholics were oppressed and persecuted during the years of the Protestant Ascendancy. For a long while Catholics were not even allowed to own a horse of more than £5 value, a bitter thing for a horse-loving people.

Gradually, the British grip on Ireland tightened. A climate of hostility developed, and Irish patriots determined to free Ireland from England's iron rule, when, as it was said, the crown was over the harp – the British crown over the Irish harp.

The Easter Rising

Many Irish folk songs are about heroes and patriots who died fighting for Ireland. They fought to make their country free; to free themselves from the British who ruled Dublin and the rest of Ireland from Dublin Castle in the heart of the city. The castle is surmounted by a huge statue of the figure of Justice, but the statue has its back to the city, and Irishmen said this meant, 'No justice for Ireland.'

A great crowd had gathered
Outside of Kilmainham

Their heads all uncovered
They knelt on the ground.
For inside that grim prison
Lay a brave Irish soldier . . .

Although the words of that song are about the heroes
of 1916, the fight for freedom had been going on much
longer than that, for it was eight centuries earlier that
Dublin came under English rule. It took the Irish
seven hundred years to free themselves from English
mastery.

Over the centuries, one rebellion followed another,
and each of them was as unsuccessful as the last. In
the nineteenth century alone there were countless
attempts to throw off English rule. These, too, failed.
Often their leaders were executed.

But in 1916 there came a rising which was to be
somehow different. One of its leaders was a school-
master, Patrick Pearse. He was a slight, fair man,
with a gift for impassioned oratory. He learned the
spirit of freedom at an early age, and remembering
his youth, he said, 'When I was a child of ten I went
down on my bare knees by my bedside one night and
promised God that I should devote my life to free my
country.' And it was with these hopes in his heart
that he grew up with his family.

Patrick Pearse became a Headmaster, and worked
to pass on to his boys the Irish language, Irish
traditions and the dream of freedom.

Pearse, and the friends he gathered round him,
formed a society called the Irish Volunteers. They
learned to use arms they brought from abroad for

Patrick Pearse

Pearse believed that without arms Ireland would only be free when it was convenient to England.

He said, 'There are many things more horrible than bloodshed – one of them is slavery.'

Posters invited people to join the Volunteers in a programme of training each Friday night. Training started with musketry at eight o'clock, and the meetings were well attended. This was 1914, and England was at war with Germany. Irishmen were asked to fight on England's side; many of them did, and fought bravely, but the new patriots would not. At their meetings they made their intentions clear: 'We fight for neither King nor Kaiser.'

Patrick Pearse and his friends formed a secret plan – to rise up and free the city of Dublin from the hated English rule. They knew that in the end the small forces could never capture Dublin from the British Army, but they longed to show the English

Joseph Plunkett

that some Irishmen were ready to fight for their country. They were prepared to die in this tremendous gesture.

He and his friends were not soldiers, not men of blood, but shopkeepers, poets, teachers and trade union leaders. William Pearse, Patrick's brother, was with them heart and soul. He was an art master at his brother's school. Joseph Plunkett was a tall, frail young man, who suffered from tuberculosis. He got up from his sick bed to join in the campaign.

The date was fixed for Easter Sunday 1916.

Because the patriots were ordinary people, not professional soldiers, they were not the best organized army in the world. Pearse sent a letter to each of his

57

men telling them what they would have to do, but his instructions were hardly adequate for a long, armed rising:—

'You will provide yourself with a bicycle, a street map of Dublin City, a road map of the district, and a Field Message Book. You will bring full arms and ammunition, full service equipment (including over-coat) and rations for eight hours.'

There was some confusion in the orders to mobilize, and in the end far fewer men turned out for Pearse than he had expected. Dublin was peaceful and un-suspecting. There were few British troops in the city because of the war with Germany. Dubliners hardly turned their heads when they heard the Volunteers marching. But this was no practice drill. The leaders fanned out through the city and occupied key points,

The GPO O'Connell Street

declaring they had captured them from the British.

Pearse marched his detachment straight into the GPO – Dublin's main Post Office in Sackville Street – and into the building. His men told the startled officials that they were taking it over. Then Patrick Pearse came out of the main door, with a piece of paper in his hands. Standing on top of the steps he read it to the people outside.

The Provisional Government of the Irish Republic.
To the People of Ireland –
Irishmen and Irishwomen – in the name of God and the dead generations – we declare the right of the people of Ireland to be sovereign.

By this piece of paper, Patrick Pearse and the other leaders who signed it declared the English mastery of Ireland at an end, and an Irish Republic founded.

Most Dubliners hardly cared.

The English were taken by surprise. They quickly rushed troops into Dublin, with munitions and armoured trucks.

Soon parts of Dublin became battlefields, as shells rained down on the patriots' buildings. The Volunteers could get no help from outside Dublin, because the city had been cut off. Their different contingents were isolated from each other in various parts of the city.

The fighting continued through that Easter week, but the Volunteers were running out of ammunition, and with only eight hours rations they had long since run out of food. The British worked methodically to crush the rising, and on the Friday the GPO was set on fire by the shelling. Patrick Pearse, Joseph Plunkett and their men were forced to leave it – Plunkett was now ill and exhausted.

After the fire, the GPO was a gutted hollow wreck, and the other strongholds of the Volunteers were destroyed or surrounded.

Then Pearse made his decision. He went before the English commander to surrender. He knew it was the only thing to do, and that to fight on would mean many of his men would be killed. He felt that surrender was the only way he could save their lives, though maybe not his own.

Dubliners were aghast at the damage that had been done to their city. They wandered round the ruined capital, bewildered and resentful. They had not asked for the Rising and were furiously angry. As the prisoners were marched through the streets they jeered and threw stones at them.

There was little hope for the leaders. Because it was war time, they were tried by army court martial. They were condemned to death, and taken to jail to await their execution. Kilmainham Jail was a maximum security jail for political prisoners. Many Irish patriots from previous risings had been imprisoned here before them.

Today Kilmainham is a Museum, open to the public. It hasn't been used as a jail for fifty years now, yet as I walked into the main hall, from which the cells opened, and looked up into the network of grilles and bars, I felt cold and wretched. I could imagine the icy chill that must have struck the hearts of the prisoners as they were brought in, leaving hope behind them.

I was shown round by the Secretary of the Museum Restoration Committee, Mr James Brennan. Today he is an old gentleman, but he was a young man in 1916, when he took part in the Rising, and was brought to Kilmainham as a prisoner.

All the cells in the condemned block have the names of the men who once occupied them painted over the door. They read like a Death Roll for most of them were executed in just over one week in 1916. Of the rest, very few are alive today, for it was fifty-seven years ago.

But Mr Brennan is still a very sprightly and cheerful old gentleman of eighty-two. He showed me into his cell like someone politely opening the door of his sitting room to an unexpected visitor.

It was a stark, dank, horrible little stone room, completely empty. I asked how much furniture there had been when he was a prisoner.

'Nothing at all – no bed, no table, no chair, no light. At night I just put my head on my boots and snoozed off!'

'Did you know your friends were being executed?'

'Oh, yes, we could hear the shots of the firing squad quite clearly. It happened very early every morning. Each time I knew one of my comrades was being shot. But of course I didn't know which one it was, until later on.'

I asked how long he waited wondering when it was going to be *his* turn.

'One day they opened that door and told me the

finding of the Court Martial was that I was sentenced to death.'

'And then what happened?' I asked.

'Well – nothing much, until later on. I hadn't expected anything else, you see. It wasn't until much later in the day they came again and opened the door, and said it had been changed to penal servitude.'

I asked if he could remember how he felt when he heard the news.

'Well, you know, it's strange. You see I had made up my mind to die for Ireland, and I was prepared for death. And when the news of the reprieve came I felt nothing but disappointment!'

All the leaders who had signed the proclamation had been condemned to death, and none of them was reprieved.

In the chapel of Kilmainham Jail, Joseph Plunkett was granted his last request. He was engaged to be married; his fiance was a beautiful and devoted girl called Grace Gifford. The day before Joseph was to be executed she was brought to the prison and at eight o'clock in the evening she and Joseph Plunkett were married in the prison chapel. Immediately after the ceremony Grace was sent away, and Joseph was taken back to his cell. They met once more, in the early hours of the next morning. Grace was again brought to the prison, and she and Joseph were allowed to talk together for ten minutes in his cell, while soldiers stood by with fixed bayonets. Then they parted. About an hour later Joseph was shot. His wife never remarried, and bore the name of Plunkett for the rest of her life.

Both the Pearse brothers were sentenced to be shot, and for them, too, there was no reprieve.

Patrick awaited his death. His last wish, to see his mother, was not granted, and the night before he died he wrote her one last letter.

My Dearest Mother,

I have been hoping up to now that it would be possible for me to see you again, but it does not seem possible.

Goodbye, dear, dear, Mother.

I have just received Holy Communion. I am happy except for the great grief of parting from you. This is the death I should have asked for if God had given me the choice of all deaths, to die a soldier's death for Ireland and for freedom.

Pearse in his cell

We have done right. People will say hard things of us now, but later on they will praise us. Do not grieve for all this, but think of it as a sacrifice which God asked of me and you.

Goodbye again, dear, dear Mother. May God bless you for your great love for me and for your great faith, and may he remember all that you have so bravely suffered. I have not words to tell of my love of you, and how my heart yearns to you all.

I will call to you in my heart at the last moment.

Your son – Pat.

The last moments in the prison yard.

The fourteen men were executed there, where high walls shut in the small yard and the shooting could not be seen from the windows of the cells. The men were not all shot at the same time, but each day for a whole week either two or three were shot at dawn. A cross stands now where the men stood, facing the firing squad opposite. The last to be shot was James Connolly – he had been badly wounded in the fighting and so he was brought to the jail in an ambulance and shot strapped to a chair.

The Rising was over and at first it seemed that it had failed.

The leaders were dead and the Republic had lasted only six days. Then a strange thing happened. News of the leaders' brave deaths quickly spread through Dublin – indeed, outside the Jail the shots could be heard every morning.

People began to feel differently about them, they

no longer jeered at the Republic as an impossible dream, but began to realize that Ireland could soon become free and independent. By that drawn out week of executions, the British themselves had made certain of the success of the Rising.

The leaders were buried in a communal grave at the Arbour Hill Cemetery. More bloodshed was to follow before the Republic of Ireland came into being, but the 1916 Rising produced an impetus which led to freedom six years later.

Patrick Pearse, William Pearse, Joseph Plunkett, James Connolly and the rest are national heroes now: their graves are honoured, and above them floats the flag of the Irish Republic they died for.

Irish children today are taught to remember them, and the words of Patrick Pearse:

'Life springs from death, and from the graves of patriot men and women spring living nations.'

CEAÓ MÍLE FÁILTE

In all my Special Assignments I've tried to show the history of the cities, and how it relates to the lives of the people who live in them today. But in Dublin the most important part of its past is very close to the present. 1916 is only fifty-eight years ago. There are people who still remember those days and those shots that rang out every morning from Kilmainham, heralding a new and independent Ireland.

Yet today Dublin is a cheerful modern city, and many Dubliners are cheerful people who are interested in the present and the future. Britain is no longer an enemy, but Ireland's equal in the new European Common Market.

A thousand welcomes – Cead Mile Failte in the old Gaelic – has become the slogan of the new Ireland!

YORK

York People

In the year three hundred and six, AD, the Roman Emperor Constantius Chlorus died in York, and in the centre of the city, where the streets of Stonegate and Petergate cross, the people crowned his son to take his place. *He* became Constantine the Great, the first Christian Emperor, and the founder of the city of Constantinople.

In fifteen hundred and seventy, Richard Fawkes brought his son for christening, to the church of St Michael le Belfrey, from his lodging across the street. Guy Fawkes later went to St Peter's School. Today it's the only school in England where bonfires are banned on November 5th – they don't burn old pupils!

In seventeen hundred and thirty-nine, a man called John Palmer was in York prison, awaiting trial for killing a chicken. Then a careless slip in a letter revealed he was really Dick Turpin the Highwayman – and the slip cost him his life. Turpin was executed outside the city, and buried in St George's churchyard.

The Capital of the North

York is full of surprises, but then it's had a long history. It's been the home of kings and emperors, of traitors and martyrs, of great pageants and great rebellions. For centuries it was the most important city outside London – the Capital of the North.

Today, it's a small city (just 100,000 inhabitants) but it still has a tremendous pull on visitors, and that's because it has preserved its past so well.

The town centre is still almost medieval in layout, with narrow streets, tiny courtyards and alleyways, and hundreds of historic buildings. What's more, the people of York have decided they want to keep it that way. The only trouble is that the traffic is very much twentieth century. York has the only bridges across the River Ouse for a dozen miles in either direction, and it's on the direct holiday route to the east coast seaside resorts. It's the classic example of a bottleneck, and one day it's just going to grind to a halt.

What about a bypass? Well, the government has plans for one, and the Corporation wants an inner ringroad. But at the moment they're only plans, and until one of them is built York will remain something of a battlefield for the motorist, with today's traffic wrestling with yesterday's streets.

But you don't need a car to see the sights of York. After all, there were no cars in the Middle Ages, and people managed to get around then. York is the ideal town for walking – and as for ringroads, it already has one for pedestrians only!

The city walls were built for defence, but they have been kept in good condition for centuries, and now they make wonderful footpaths, a nice twenty feet

The Walls of York

above the traffic. It takes about an hour and a half to walk round, and I found it a marvellous way to get to know the city, its chequered history, and its four different names.

The city was founded by the Roman Army in AD 671, and they called it Eboracum. Parts of their fortress wall have been carefully excavated, and show that the ground level was probably about twenty feet lower then than it is today. The Romans abandoned

Eboracum early in the fifth century, and were replaced by the Anglo Saxons, who called it Eforwic. Under their rule it became a centre of Christianity and scholarship – one Saxon scholar, Alcuin, was famous throughout Europe.

Then came the Danes, and they changed the name to Jorvik. They made it an important trading centre, too, and it's no coincidence that the shopping streets still have Scandinavian names. Goodramgate is named after the Danish King Guthrum – and there are plenty of others.

1066 brought the Normans to Jorvik, and they began by burning it down to stop a rebellion. But they were great builders as well as soldiers, and within fifty years a new city, now called York, had risen from the ruins of the old.

It had a castle, it had new walls – but, above all, it had churches, dozens of them. There was St Denys, St Margaret, St Martin-cum-Gregory, St Martin le Grand, St Michael, All Saints, St Mary, St John. At one time there were forty churches within the city walls – there are still twenty today.

York Minster

The Normans also set about rebuilding the old Saxon Church at the north end of Stonegate, and so laid the foundations of the present York Minster.

Why is it called a Minster, I wondered, why not York Cathedral? It *is* a cathedral, because it's the seat of the Archbishop of York, but it's a Minster, too, because it was a centre of Christian learning.

The word minster is used all over Yorkshire for really important churches.

And York was important. It's the largest Gothic church in the country, and it dominates the city of

York Minster

York. Wherever you are, you find yourself looking for its tall graceful tower, that seems to be soaring right up into the sky, and the mass of the pale grey stonework.

Margaret Clitherow

It's easy to imagine, seeing how the Minster still dominates the tiny medieval streets, how important religion was to the people who built and decorated it. For a thousand years the Minster was the heart of York, and the life of the church dominated the lives of its townspeople. Church and town were bound together, and when there was discord in the church the townspeople felt it.

When a break came, it came violently, just fifty years after the Minster was completed. The English Church was shaken to its foundations when Henry VIII decided to break away from the church of Rome. By the time his daughter Elizabeth was queen, the majority of English people had decided to take the Protestant side, and laws were passed to forbid Catholic services. But there remained some who wished to worship in the old Catholic way, who felt that to be disloyal to the Pope and to the old Church was heresy.

They held services in their homes, though this was dangerous. Priests especially were at risk. They went about the country with a price on their heads facing imprisonment or even death if they were caught taking services for groups of Catholics in secret. Householders built secret hiding places, called Priests' Holes, where the priest could hide if non-catholic visitors called. I went to a house in Stonegate, to see the priest's hole there.

But what if a family was divided? This was the situation that faced a young woman called Margaret Clitherow. Her husband was a Protestant, she wished to be Catholic. In trying to solve her problem Margaret became one of the few English women to be martyred, and later to be made a saint.

She lived in a street called The Shambles, where the butchers used to have their shops. The hooks for hanging meat, and the ledges for displaying it, are still there. Margaret's husband John was a butcher, a prosperous and respected citizen, and of course his shop was there. Today that shop has been made into a shrine to Margaret's memory.

It was in 1574 that Margaret was converted to the Catholic faith. She decided that she could not accept the Queen as Head of the Church, with the right to order its beliefs and services, and she refused to attend the parish church in Coney Street where she and John had been married just three years before. Her husband was understanding, though he did not share her views, and agreed that their three children should have a Catholic schoolteacher, and be given secret lessons in the attic of their house.

He turned a blind eye when occasionally Margaret hid a Catholic priest there. His name was Father John Mush, and he was later to write down the story of her life. He often warned her she was putting her husband and friends at risk, but she replied, 'If God's priests dare venture themselves to my house, I will never refuse them!'

For Margaret knew that all Catholic priests were in constant danger; the law was severe. To deny that the Queen was head of the Church was treason, and treason was punished with a horrible death on the Tyburn gallows outside the city walls at Knavesmire.

Already a number of priests had been executed, and to the Catholics of York they were martyrs. The place where they had died was holy ground. Often Margaret walked out at night, careful not to be seen, to spend an hour in silent prayer in the very place where they had suffered.

73

Then, in 1585, the English Parliament, fearful of Catholic plots to assassinate Queen Elizabeth, passed an even harsher law. It condemned not only priests, but anyone who helped or hid them, to the traitors' death. The Catholics of York did not know what would happen next to any of them. Father Mush told Margaret, 'You must prepare your neck for the rope!'

'God's will be done,' she answered. 'But I am far unworthy of that honour. I do not see in myself any worthiness of martyrdom!'

Some weeks later, John Clitherow was called to the Sheriff's office for questioning – and while he was gone, two sergeants arrived to search the house. Downstairs there was nothing to be seen, but Margaret knew that upstairs the schoolteacher, Mr Stapleton, was giving a lesson to her children and one or two others.

She led the soldiers upstairs with a heavy heart, but in the attic they found only the children. Mr Stapleton had heard the noise downstairs, and had escaped through a small door on to the roof. Margaret breathed a sigh of relief, but she had forgotten one thing. Father John Mush had been in the house the week before, and had left behind his vestments, and the bread and wine necessary to say Mass.

The soldiers seized the children and threatened them. One of them – not Margaret's – was frightened into leading the men to the hiding place. It was enough evidence for the Sheriff's men. Margaret was arrested, and ordered to stand her trial.

On March 14th she was taken to York's Guildhall.

It must have looked very different from the many times she had gone there with her husband to attend official banquets.

'Margaret Clitherow,' she heard the Judge say, 'You are accused of harbouring priests, traitors to the Queen's Majesty and her laws, and of hearing Mass. Do you plead Guilty or Not Guilty?'

She had thought out this problem. She could not say Guilty, for she did not believe the priests to be traitors. But if she pleaded Not Guilty the trial would go forward, and evidence might be given that would harm her friends and her husband. She refused to plead. 'Having made no offence, I need no trial.'

This caused consternation. In those days, people could only be tried by jury if they agreed to plead. If they refused, the law said they must be submitted to the ordeal – they were tortured until they agreed to a trial, or until they died.

The Judges were furious, but Margaret stood firm. 'I will be tried by none but by God and your own consciences,' she told them.

The justices now realized they were in an impossible situation. 'If she is allowed to live,' said one, 'there will be more of her kind without any fear of the law.' Another pointed out that if she were acquitted, every criminal, thief and murderer would refuse to plead. They had no alternative but to condemn her to the ordeal, and, since they knew that she would never change her mind, to certain death.

They told her what heavy penalties were inflicted on prisoners who refused to plead. 'We must proceed by law against you, which will condemn you to a sharp death for want of trial.'

'God's will be done,' she answered. 'I thank God I may suffer any death for this good cause.'

All the onlookers noticed how calm – even cheerful – she was, when the sentence was read out, with the dreadful death traditionally imposed on people who would not accept the Queen's Court.

As she was led from the Guildhall through the streets of York, where she had lived all the thirty years of her life, the cobbles were crowded with people who knew her. She was taken down to the river and then, secretly, by boat downstream to the Ouse Bridge Prison. She had hoped she might die on the gallows at Knavesmire, like the other Catholic martyrs, but the justices feared possible protests. Margaret and her husband were popular in the city.

She was executed on March 25th, 1586, Good Friday. Only a few witnesses were allowed to be present, but from them Father John Mush pieced together an account of all that happened:

'When the time came, there were present the two Sheriffs, a minister, four sergeants and four women. The Sheriff said, "Mrs Clitherow, you must remember and confess that you die for treason."

"No, no, Master Sheriff," said Margaret. "I die for the love of my Lord Jesus."

She was ordered to take off all her clothes – the other women begged that she need not do this, but it was not granted. So the women helped her to undress, and to put on a short linen tunic. She was ordered to lie down on the floor; very quietly, she did so, and her face was covered with a handkerchief. A heavy oak door was laid on top of her, and her hands and feet bound to posts. After this they laid heavy weights upon the door, which when she first felt, she cried, "Jesus, have mercy on me!" – which were the last words she was heard to speak.'

I heard the end of the story in a house in York, which became a Convent just one hundred years after Margaret died.

Her body was buried hurriedly by the sergeants in some waste ground, but six weeks later some Catholics discovered the grave. They re-buried the body, so secretly that it was never found, but as a precious relic of their martyr they took one of the hands, and embalmed it.

Today it is preserved with loving care in the York Bar Convent, where I went to see it.

I must admit there was a large part of me that wasn't actually looking forward to seeing a hand cut from the body of a woman who had died in agony in the sixteenth century. But another part of me was frankly curious. I went along with the Blue Peter crew to the Bar Convent, a lovely old building just outside the city walls, which is why it is called the 'Bar' convent.

We were met by Sister Amadeus, a kindly round-faced Yorkshire nun, who took us through to the room where the hand is kept. Sister Amadeus went to a little curtained cupboard in the wall. She drew aside the curtain, and brought out something covered by a veil. Under the veil was a domed glass

77

case, containing what many people believe to be the hand of St Margaret Clitherow.

Strangely enough, it wasn't spooky at all. It was dark brown, and looked almost as though it was made of wax, but it *was*, unmistakably, a small fragile human hand, with the fingers oddly tense and curled, like the hand of someone in great pain.

I asked Sister Amadeus how the relic came to be in the possession of the Sisters of the Bar Convent. She began to rearrange the veil over the hand.

'Well, we're not exactly sure how we got hold of it, but we *do* know that a priest called Father John Mush who wrote the Life of Margaret Clitherow was a friend of another great Yorkshire woman called Mary Ward, who became our foundress. So it seems that that is the connection. Exactly whom it was given to, and on what date, we don't know for certain at all.'

I asked Sister Amadeus how long Margaret Clitherow had been a saint. She placed the hand back in its cupboard, carefully arranged the curtain that concealed it, and said: 'Only since 1970. It takes an awful long time to make a saint, you know. After years and years of studying her life, they proclaimed that she really was a saint, because she had followed Our Lord's life very, very closely whilst she lived, and now she is happily in Heaven. They made her a saint to be an example to us, to help us to be as strong a Christian as she was.'

Margaret Clitherow and the martyred priests were not the only victims of the Reformation. The Protestants disliked any form of religious pageantry, and frowned upon the medieval mystery plays. They were performed in 1575, eleven years before Margaret's death, but then they were banned. Now, four centuries later, they have been revived.

Once every three years, since 1931, York has celebrated a Festival of the Arts. It's a mixture of all kinds of entertainment, ranging from organ recitals in the Minster to informal 'happenings' in the streets, but the main attraction has always been the Mystery Plays. They were first performed in York 600 years ago, and during the Festival two of the York schools mount one in the traditional way – on a waggon.

All the plays tell stories from the Bible, and when I was there it was the play about the Three Wise Men and King Herod.

> *And so that ye the sooth will say,*
> *To come and go I grant you grace,*
> *And if your point so please me may*
> *Maybe myself will wend you with ...*

declaimed the boy who was King Herod, to the crowd gathered round the cart.

> *Sir King, we all accord*
> *And say a bairn is born,*
> *That shall be King and Lord*
> *And heal them that are lorn ...*

replied the Wise Men.

I found that I could understand the dialogue quite well, but one thing struck me as peculiar. A lot of the lines are written with as many words as possible beginning with the same letter. This was obviously an accepted style in the fourteenth century, although today most playwrights would avoid it. The play went on:

> *Hail, flower fairest that never shall fade!*
> *Hail, son, that is sent of this same seed*
> *That shall save us from sins that our sires made.*
> *Hail, mild, whose measure shall mark us our meed,*
> *Of a maid matchless thy mother thou made . . .*

The play lasts about twenty minutes, and by the end, despite the busy York traffic, it had gathered a large audience.

Even today most of the plays are known by the name of the guild who performed them – and the guilds tried to do a play that reflected their trade. For instance, the Last Supper was done by the bakers, because they could supply the bread. The play about the Marriage Feast at Cana was done by the wine merchants. As for the play about Noah and the Flood, the Shipwrights wanted to do it, but so did the Fishermen, *and* the Mariners!

The richest guild, the Merchant Adventurers, was responsible for the Day of Judgement, as this required a waggon with trap doors and other expensive extras. And the first play in the cycle – The Creation – was entrusted to the Barkers, to make sure everyone heard the lines.

It would be impossible nowadays to put the full set of plays on, in the medieval manner – the traffic jam would be enormous! But the people of York have thought of a good way of showing what the Cycle of Mystery Plays was like. A selection of the forty-eight plays is performed in the grounds of St Mary's Abbey every evening, and a large stand is erected to hold the hundreds of visitors. The performance covers the whole Bible story, from the Creation to the Day of Judgement, and the cast list, though not quite three hundred and fifty, is still enormous.

In this setting, I found I could really begin to understand the feelings of the unknown men who wrote the plays six centuries ago, with the citizens of York for their actors and their audience.

The Railway King

Today, York is a 'Railway Town'. For centuries the narrow streets and huddled houses kept the city in the Middle Ages, but the coming of the steam engine hauled York into modern times. How did it come about? In the 1830s, when the railways began, York had no industry, no coal, no great population.

What it did have was one of the greatest railway enthusiasts of all time, and to trace his story I followed the train ten miles out of York to the village of Howsham. It's just a single street of cottages, and it can't have changed much since 1800, when George Hudson was born. His father was a prosperous farmer, but George had greater ambitions. At the end of the street stood Howsham Hall, and he was determined that one day he would own such a mansion.

When he was fifteen he left for York to seek his fortune. He was apprenticed in a big linen-draper's business. Energetic, ambitious and determined to get on, by the time he was twenty-one he had married the boss's daughter and become a partner in the firm. For six years he was a successful shopkeeper. Years later, he said, 'I would be a better man today if I had never left that little shop,' but at the time he thought differently, he longed to jump over his shop counter and get out into the world.

Then a rich uncle left him £30,000 in his will. George looked for ways to invest his fortune. He wanted more money, and power and influence too. He found them all in two things that then went hand in hand: politics and railways.

The iron road was still a novelty. The first railway lines were being laid, the first trains were making their way across the country. Money for them was difficult to find, so the York Railway Committee welcomed George with open arms, and made him their Chairman. At the same time the City Council wanted a rich chairman, and they made him Lord Mayor. In 1837 he took up residence in the Mansion House, and his rise to power began.

On May 29th, 1839, the first railway line out of York was opened, with exuberant festivities. A huge breakfast was held in the Mansion House, and then four hundred distinguished passengers crowded into the two engines and nineteen carriages of the new train. A bell rang, a whistle blew, and the train hurtled away at twenty miles an hour. Then back to York, to the Guildhall, for an enormous banquet, which began at half past four and went on until ten. George Hudson made a speech in which he promised to, 'make *All* the railways come to York.' Then everyone went to the Mansion House for a dance that lasted until four in the morning.

George Hudson

Breathless and overwhelmed by all the excitement, the people of York presented a testimonial to Lord Mayor George Hudson, thanking him for 'the able, satisfactory and munificent manner in which he has most materially promoted the honour of the city and the best interests of its citizens.'

The delighted Council proposed that his portrait should be hung in the Mansion House. It is there today, looking just as a reporter described it in one newspaper, 'He is about five feet eight inches in height, with a short burly neck. His face attracts attention, and the expression of his eyes is most peculiar.' For some reason, the reporter went on, 'At first sight one dislikes him!'

But, likeable or not, there was no doubt he could build railways, and soon he showed he could out-smart his rivals, too. His first line stretched from York to Leeds and Hudson himself walked over all the fields it would cross, and arranged to buy up every yard of land it would need. Fifteen miles out of York it crossed another line, which ran from Selby to Leeds. Hudson was determined this should not compete with *his* line, so he bought control of the Leeds and Selby Railway, and closed it to passenger trains. Travellers now had to change at Milford Junction, and go the Hudson way, even though it took longer!

He was a master of railway finance. No one person, not even he, had enough money to build a railway, but people could share – each put up some of the money, share the risks, and hope to share the profits. They got share certificates – pieces of paper saying they had paid money to take part in the railway venture.

This is a share certificate for the York and North Midland Railway, signed by George Hudson.

YORK AND NORTH MIDLAND RAILWAY.

SCARBROUGH EXTENSION CERTIFICATE.

ONE SHARE OF £25.

ON WHICH A DEPOSIT OF £2, 10s. HAS BEEN PAID.

The holder of this Certificate will be entitled to ONE SHARE in the YORK and NORTH MIDLAND RAILWAY COMPANY, for the SCARBROUGH EXTENSION, when the Act of Parliament shall have been obtained.

Jso Hudson

CHAIRMAN OF THE BOARD OF DIRECTORS.

YORK, 1st JANUARY, 1844.

No. 651

SECRETARY.

Railway Share Certificate

By manipulating share money, Hudson built railways so quickly that no one had time to question his methods. At company meetings he inspired complete confidence with glowing reports of increased business and profits and by 1844 he controlled most of the railways in the Midlands. By 1846 his network stretched from Bristol in the South West to Newcastle in the North East. In 1848 he was running one third of all the railways in Britain, a total of 1,500 miles, and people hailed him 'The Railway King'.

The King bought his palace, too, Baldersby Park, twenty miles north of York. Here George achieved his childhood dream, and became a landed gentleman. He bought a splendid house in London, too, and all the great people of the day flocked to visit him. He was presented to Queen Victoria; even the

Duke of Wellington sought his advice on railway matters. He became a Member of Parliament, and used his influence to push through every measure to do with the railways that would benefit him and his followers.

Perhaps his finest hour came on June 10th, 1847, when he escorted Queen Victoria and Prince Albert to Cambridge. The newspapers – and the Queen – were ecstatic.

'On entering the reception room where the Chairman and Directors awaited their arrival, Her Majesty very condescendingly bade Mr Hudson Good Morning. On observing all the preparations made for her journey, Her Majesty remarked in evident delight, "Really, this is beautiful! Is it not most gratifying?" '

But York, his home city, was still important to him. Three times he was Lord Mayor – the Dick Whittington of York – and lived in the Mansion House, where he was renowned for his lavish hospitality.

'Mr Hudson,' said one admirer, 'is the sort of man who *ought* to be rich. He has provided business for the citizen, employment for labour, trade for the shopkeeper, and markets for our manufactures.'

But in 1848 everything changed. There were revolutions in Europe, trade suffered, and the mania for railways came to a halt.

The truth was that Hudson had been spending money he didn't have. He'd pretended his companies were making good profits, when actually many were losing badly. He had been like a juggler, somehow keeping all the complicated enterprises spinning in the air, while the audience gazed spellbound. But in juggling, once one object falls, the act is over, and the juggler is booed off the stage!

The half-yearly meeting of the York, Newcastle and Berwick Railway took place in the Assembly Rooms in York on February 20th, 1849. Hudson was in the chair, but before he could give his report Mr Horatio Love, a London accountant, rose to ask a question. 'Mr Hudson, have you ever altered the figures in the yearly accounts?'

Hudson was taken aback, but replied quickly, 'I may have carried forward one or two thousand to the following year.'

'Did you ever carry forward £10,000?'

Hudson was flabbergasted, but his questioner went on relentlessly, insisting that Hudson must have falsified accounts, concealing vast sums of money from the other shareholders. And there was no record, he claimed, of anything that Hudson had done. He had been responsible for other people's money, and could not – or would not – say what he had done with it all.

All that was now Hudson's undoing. All his companies began to examine their accounts, and found very little there. They suspected that Hudson had deceived them, and there was nothing to prove otherwise. He had made many enemies in thirteen years of railway politics, and no one came to save him now.

Within a year he was a ruined man, many of his companies bankrupt, his land and houses up for sale.

York tried to forget his existence. A street had been named after him – now it was re-named 'Railway

Street'. Money subscribed for a statue was used to erect one of his greatest political rival, George Leeman. The Mansion House portrait was removed to the cellar. Friends and relations deserted him, and for the next twenty-one years he lived obscure and forgotten.

But one relation did remain loyal – his nephew William. He collected mementos of his uncle's 'reign', and handed them down to his family. William's grandson, Henry Hudson, still lives in York, and I went to visit him in his modest comfortable house on the outskirts of the town. He looks remarkably like the pictures of his great-great uncle George, but he doesn't live in the extravagant manner of the Railway King. He proudly showed me the magnificent and enormous carving set presented to George by the Master Cutlers of Sheffield. I admired the inlaid railway train running along the length of the blade, and the effigy of Hudson himself carved on the ivory handles, and I asked Henry Hudson if he ever used them. He looked wistfully at the huge gleaming knife, and said, 'No. My joints are a bit too small for a knife like that.'

I asked him if the family had felt shocked when the crunch came.

'Oh, no, we were very proud of him – both my father and my grandfather. I mean, after all, he did a tremendous lot to speed up the railways, whatever else he did.' He glanced up at the great gilt-framed picture of the man he so much ressembled, and said, 'All great men make mistakes!'

The last thing he showed me was a letter written by his great-great-uncle to his grandfather.

My dear William,

I arrived back here on Saturday about eight pm. I was very poorly on my arrival. I sent for Dr Mattheson, who blistered and applied other remedies.

I hope your little Goerge is better. I should like to hear from you about him.

Your affectionate uncle
George Hudson.

Hudson died at last in London in 1871. Many people had forgotten him, but *The Times* passed fair judgement in its obituary: 'George Hudson was placed in a novel situation of great power. If he had behaved with perfect fairness he would have been little less than an angel, and that he certainly was not.'

Hudson's body was brought back to his own city by rail. A funeral procession from the station wound over the Lendal Road Bridge, which had at last been opened, while the bells of the Minster and the City churches were tolled and many citizens thought back to the stormy, puzzling reign of the Railway King. The procession reached the parish where he had been born, and the little churchyard of Scrayingham. In a plain undistinguished grave the story of George Hudson came to an end – or very nearly.

A hundred years is a long time to bear ill-will, and the lines Hudson built are still bringing people and trade to York. British Rail were the first to weaken – they decided to name their new headquarters building 'Hudson House'. Then, on the centenary of Hudson's death, the York Civic Trust proclaimed, 'There is no doubt that George Hudson brought to the City a lasting and important place in the life of the railways of this country. We should make an end to his disgrace.' So York also relented, and after a hundred and twenty-two years Railway Street became Hudson Street once more.

Today, York can accept George Hudson for what he was. In his day he was a bully and a profiteer, neither likeable nor honest. But he spread the railways everywhere, and made York the railway town that it still is. Perhaps York can, once again, in the words of the original testimonial, offer thanks to George Hudson, 'for the able, satisfactory and munificent manner in which he has most materially promoted the honour of the City, and the best interests of its citizens.'

The Castle Museum

While I was in York, I was determined to seize the chance of visiting a favourite place of mine – the Castle Museum.

On Blue Peter we had often been allowed to borrow strange and fascinating things for the programme from this museum – I remembered a very early vacuum cleaner, and an extraordinary washing machine! And once we had come here with the Blue Peter cameras, to make a film. I had always wanted to come back for a good look round, because I was certain the whole collection would be quite amazing.

It certainly was!

It is housed in two elegant and beautiful buildings,

designed, in the first place, for two prisons, part of the complex of buildings that made up York Castle.

Inside, it is not like some museums, with rows of articles in show cases, or on display shelves, in a dry-as-dust atmosphere. This Museum is full of bustling life. There is a cobbled street, lined with Victorian shops, stocked with everything they would have had to sell in Victorian times. There is a Victorian parlour, a Jacobean hall, a moorland cottage. Every shop and every house is full of the exact items that should be there, in the right place. There are ornaments over the fireplace, china on the table, and ploughs and grindstones in the barn.

It is a real trip back into the living past.

Mr Patterson, the Curator, an old friend of Blue Peter, was delighted when he saw how amazed I was.

'It's a marvellous collection,' I said, 'But I just don't understand how it has all come together, and why it is displayed so magnificently.'

'It's a long story,' he told me, 'and to understand it we ought to go twenty miles outside York, to a little market town called Pickering.'

So we drove out into the country, and stopped by a big house just off the main road.

'This is Houndgate House,' said Mr Patterson. 'Sixty years ago John Kirk lived here. He was the local doctor, but medicine wasn't his only interest. He was an amateur photographer, and a racing car enthusiast, and he had the greatest passion for collecting I have ever known.'

As I looked at the house and garden, I thought they looked rather strange. The house was decorated with gargoyles, and in the middle of the garden stood a pinnacle like a church spire. 'Did he collect those?' I asked.

'Oh, yes. There used to be a moorland cross here as well, but that has gone back to its own village. But of course, when Dr Kirk lived here, the garden was full of things.'

'What kind of things?'

'Anything from the past, that people had actually used as part of their daily lives in a bygone age,' the Curator said. 'On his medical visits he would go into cottages, and farms, and big houses, and see kitchen equipment, and farm implements, or furniture and ornaments, and often the owners thought they were all just so much junk. So Dr Kirk begged them to give the things to him. Sometimes he asked for them instead of the money to settle his bills. So his collection grew and grew.'

'Wherever did he put it all?' I wondered.

'At first, in the garden, and in the building he called the Motor House. His own car stood outside because he had acquired a hearse, two fire engines and a hansom cab! Then he started putting things in the house, at first just in the cellars and the attics. But now people knew about him, and he was given more and more things. As you can see, it's a big house – there are about ten rooms. So he persuaded his wife to let him use one of the rooms as a museum.'

'Did she agree?'

'Oh, yes, she didn't mind his having *one* room. It was after he had taken over all the rooms but one, which they used as a bed-sitting room, that she felt it had all gone too far!'

'Whatever was the end of it all?'

'By 1930, Dr Kirk was ill, and he was getting old. He was very anxious to keep his collection together, so he offered it to Pickering District Council. They were very nice about it, and told him he could put it on the top floor of the Pickering Memorial Hall. So Dr Kirk started moving in, but then one day an official said the Hall would be needed for a Women's Institute Dance, so would he mind moving his things? So everything had to come back to Houndgate House.'

'What did he do next?'

'He advertised in a paper called the *Museum Journal*. He said "FOR DISPOSAL – One collection of Bygones and Antiquities – FREE!" He had several inquiries, but the most suitable came from York, only twenty miles away.'

'So the Collection became the Castle Museum?'

'Eventually. At first he was given one room in the disused Women's Prison, part of the Castle Buildings, but it was soon clear that it wouldn't be nearly big enough, and soon it spread to the whole building, and the old Debtors' Prison as well.'

'Did Dr Kirk have anything to do with it, after the move?'

'He certainly did. He was made Honorary Director, and he was encouraged to plan for the future. He had the imagination to design a completely new sort of museum, for nothing like it had ever been thought of before.'

We went back to York, to the Castle Museum, and I was more impressed than ever by the reality and the humanity of it all.

Mr Patterson had arranged for me to meet someone who knew the Museum in its very earliest days. He was Mr John Goodall, and forty years ago he worked on painting the Museum, and decorating the shop fronts and street signs. He told me that every Sunday evening he and the carpenter used to go to see Dr Kirk, who was often ill and in bed. They would sit down beside him, and chat about all sorts of things, and then suddenly Dr Kirk would stop, and tell them what he wanted done in the Museum during the next week.

This went on until 1938, when the Castle Museum opened. From the first it has been a fantastic success, and the whole concept of museums and exhibitions has changed because of York's Castle Museum, and Dr Kirk's ideas. No wonder that there is a plaque in the Museum, recalling Dr Kirk, who died in 1940, and who, 'Preserved for future generations a vivid picture of the everyday life of the past.'

The Past and the Future

But that is not the end. York has plans for a Folk Park, a kind of giant open-air museum, where a whole village can be assembled out of doors, and visitors can walk through life-size farm buildings, and workshops, and see items that are too big even for the Castle Museum.

One exhibit is already in place, and working away.

Raindale Mill came from near Pickering. It has been re-erected at Castle Mills Bridge, where the corn mill of York stood in the middle ages. Now a water wheel, fourteen feet in diameter, drives the shaft which turns the massive millstone and grinds the flour, just as it did when the Mill was first built in 1800. I watched fascinated as the water from the River Foss poured over the vast turning wheel, and I thought how right it was that York should have this splendid Museum where the past is preserved.

For York itself is a living museum, and you are conscious of its two thousand years of history in every building and every street, linking the past to the present. And yet, when I went about York, and met its people, and talked to the craftsmen and school-children, the railwaymen, the clergy and the citizens, I felt quite certain that York has also got a great future.

Other Books in this Series